I0158448

Madame Tricastin
Amédée

Children, Attendants, Soldiers, c.

SCENE:—A City in France, about sixty miles from the Capital.

TIME OF REPRESENTATION:—One day

THE MASSACRE

A TRAGEDY

ACT I

SCENE I

A Saloon in the house of Eusèbe Tricastin

Enter **MADAME TRICASTIN**.

MADAME TRICASTIN
What misers are we all of our real pleasures! I condemn avarice; and yet, was gold half so precious to me as the society of my dear Eusèbe Tricastin, I should be most avaricious! Even now I grudge, to a degree of rancour, my nearest, dearest relations the pleasure of his company; and think the loss of him, for one day only, beyond the appointed time of his return, a robbery on my happiness not to be forgiven.

[The door opens, and she goes hastily to meet the person entering: but, on perceiving it is **TRICASTIN Senior**, she turns away with chagrin.

TRICASTIN Snr
What, daughter, sorry to see me! This is the first time, since I have had the joy to use that name, that you have ever met me with coolness—nay, this is something more—'tis with repugnance.

MADAME TRICASTIN
Nor ought you to be offended if it is; for I was vexed at seeing you, because I hoped, as the door opened, it was your son.

TRICASTIN Snr
Ay, I imagined as much—uneasy, because he has exceeded his promise a few hours.

MADAME TRICASTIN
A few hours! half a day, and a whole night; he promised to be at home by noon yesterday.

TRICASTIN Snr
And now pray tell me—is this the first promise he has ever broken with you?

MADAME TRICASTIN
The first, either as a lover or a husband.

TRICASTIN Snr
He is then a more faithful lover and husband than ever his father was.

MADAME TRICASTIN
And you cannot be surprised, Sir, if I feel, on this occasion, such an alarm—such a despondency—

TRICASTIN Snr
For shame!—you have nothing to apprehend. Consider, my dear, he is with your mother, your uncles, your brothers, nieces and nephews; and, as he does not go from this town to Paris above once in a year—

MADAME TRICASTIN
It is still cruel of him to remain there without accounting to me for it—it is cruel of him to find delight in the society of his friends, while he knows what must be the inquietude of my mind at his stay.

TRICASTIN Snr
Cruel! And now do you suppose that my son, and your husband—he, who loved you for five years before marriage, and has adored you for ten years since—do you suppose that he could be cruel to you?

MADAME TRICASTIN
I firmly suppose he could not; and, therefore, I suffer the greatest alarm lest some accident—

TRICASTIN Snr
Here comes his friend, and yours: I met them, about two hours ago, taking a ride on the Paris road; and they told me they should go as far as the hill, in hopes to see his carriage at a distance, and be the first to bring the news to you.

MADAME TRICASTIN
Did they then know of my anxiety? I did not tell them.

TRICASTIN Snr
Tell!—is there cause for telling when a woman of sensibility loves or hates? when she feels hopes or fears, joy or sorrow? No—the passions dwell upon her every feature—none but the female hypocrite need fly to the tongue to express them.

[Enter **CONRAD** and **AMÉDÉE**.

TRICASTIN Snr
Well, have you had the good fortune to meet my son?

The Massacre by Mrs Inchbald

TAKEN FROM THE FRENCH

A TRAGEDY OF THREE ACTS

Elizabeth Simpson was born on 15th October 1753 at Stanningfield, near Bury St Edmunds, Suffolk.

Despite the fact that she suffered from a debilitating stammer she was determined to become an actress.

In April 1772, Elizabeth left, without permission, for London to pursue her chosen career. Although she was successful in obtaining parts her audiences, at first, found it difficult to admire her talents given her speech impediment. However, Elizabeth was diligent and hard-working on attempting to overcome this hurdle. She spent much time concentrating on pronunciation in order to eliminate the stammer. Her acting, although at times stilted, especially in monologues, gained praise for her approach for her well-developed characters.

That same year she married Joseph Inchbald and a few months later they appeared for the first time together on stage in 'King Lear'. The following month they toured Scotland with the West Digges's theatre company. This was to continue for several years.

Completely unexpectedly Joseph died in June 1779. It was now in the years after her husband's death that Elizabeth decided on a new literary path. With no attachments and acting taking up only some of her time she decided to write plays.

Her first play to be performed was 'A Mogul Tale or, The Descent of the Balloon', in 1784, in which she also played the leading female role of Selina. The play was premiered at the Haymarket Theatre.

One of the things that separated Elizabeth from other contemporary playwrights was her ability to translate plays from German and French into English for an audience that was ever-hungry for new works.

Her success as a playwright enabled Elizabeth to support herself and have no need of a husband to support her. Between 1784 and 1805 she had 19 of her comedies, sentimental dramas, and farces (many of them translations from the French) performed at London theatres. She is usually credited as Mrs Inchbald.

Mrs Elizabeth Inchbald died on 1st August 1821 in Kensington, London.

Index of Contents

ADVERTISEMENT

The writer of the following pages, in laying them before the public, imagines that no further reason requires to be alleged for their not having first been produced at one of our theatres, than the reason assigned by Mr. Horace Walpole (now Lord Orford) in the postscript to his much-admired tragedy, 'The Mysterious Mother,' which was never intended for representation:—From the time that I first undertook the foregoing scenes, I never flattered myself that they would be proper to appear on the stage. The subject is so horrid, that I thought it would shock, rather than give satisfaction, to an audience. Still, I found it so truly tragic in the essential springs of terror and pity, that I could not resist the impulse of adapting it to the scene, though it never could be practicable to produce it there. - Postscript to 'The Mysterious Mother.'

Having applied a paragraph of the noble author's above mentioned, to the present piece, the writer also avers, that the story of this play (as well as that of 'The Mysterious Mother') is founded upon circumstances which have been related as facts, and which the unhappy state of a neighbouring nation does but too powerfully give reason to credit.

DRAMATIS PERSONAE
MEN
Tricastin
Eusèbe Tricastin
Glandève
Rochelle
Conrad
Menancourt
Dugas
Guret
Thevenin
Clevard
Domestic
First Follower
Second Follower
WOMEN

[AMÉDÉE throws herself on a couch, nearly fainting—CONRAD shows in his manner marks of confusion and concern.

TRICASTIN Snr
What, have not you happened of him?

MADAME TRICASTIN
But they seem to have met with something—
[Going to CONRAD]
—oh! do not distract me, but tell me what it is?

CONRAD
Nothing—I hope, nothing.

MADAME TRICASTIN
Hope!—if you hope, then you also fear.

TRICASTIN Snr [Going to her]
Don't, my dear daughter, suffer yourself to be thus terrified. Do you think, if there was any cause to fear for your husband's safety, I should not be equally concerned with yourself? Why, I have known him longer than you have done, and (I could almost say) love him something better than even you do. You have other comforts; your youth, your beauty, and your many near relations: I can boast none of these—he is the only comfort I have on earth.

MADAME TRICASTIN
But, Sir, you have so much fortitude!

TRICASTIN Snr
I grant you I showed fortitude when my wife died—most men are philosophers on such an occasion; but should any accident befall my son, you would see me weak as yourself.

MADAME TRICASTIN [Going to AMÉDÉE]
Amédée, whatever makes you look thus pale, do not be afraid to tell it me.

CONRAD [In a low voice to TRICASTIN Snr]
Permit me to speak a word to you alone.

TRICASTIN Snr
Alone?—Why? Wherefore?
[Trembling]
I protest you alarm me, almost as much as my daughter is alarmed!

CONRAD [Still in a low voice]
Follow me into another room.

TRICASTIN Snr
But, if I do, her friend will tell her the secret.

CONRAD
She has promised me she will not.

TRICASTIN Snr
Don't mind her promise; she can't help it. However, I'll go with you.

[Going.

MADAME TRICASTIN
Sir! Conrad! Whither are you both going? Oh! whatever has befallen my husband, do not conceal it from me.

CONRAD
I do not know that any thing has befallen him—upon my word of honour I speak the truth.

MADAME TRICASTIN
Then why these terrifying looks? Why—

[Enter **MENANCOURT** hastily.

MENANCOURT
Tricastin, is your son returned from Paris? all his friends are trembling for his safety, and have sent me to inquire.

CONRAD
Then 'tis in vain to conceal any longer the fatal news that was told us, as we went on the road to meet him—the same accounts have now reached the town, and, I suppose, are made public.

[**MADAME TRICASTIN** throws herself on **AMÉDÉE'S** shoulder.

TRICASTIN Snr
You distract me with suspense! Tell me the worst.

MENANCOURT
Horrid disasters have fallen upon the capital—such—
[Faltering]
—as I cannot repeat.

CONRAD
Infernal massacre has been dealt to all our hapless party—bonds, vows, oaths, have been violated; nor even the prison-walls been a sanctuary for the ill-fated objects of suspicion. The report that's brought speaks of children torn from the breast of their mothers, husbands from the arms of their wives, and aged parents from their agonizing families.

TRICASTIN Snr [Stifling his grief, and taking hold of his **DAUGHTER**]
My child—we will still hope—that in pity to us all—in pity to the pangs which are else preparing for you and me—he has been spared.—Perhaps he had left the place before—who knows—

[Weeping]
—who knows, but we may see him again.

MADAME TRICASTIN [Kneeling]
Oh, grant it Heaven! Grant that I may see him once again—and living. Though wounded, mangled, dying, yet once more, let me behold him living—Let me hang over his death-bed, and, while his sense is undisturbed, tell him how much I love him, and will continue to love his memory—how I will be a tender mother to his children—and all, all, that my poor heart swells to have him know!

AMÉDÉE [Raising her]
Oh, give place to hope—you will see him again.

[Enter **EUSÈBE TRICASTIN** pale, his hair dishevelled, and his looks disordered.

MADAME TRICASTIN
I do. I do see him again.

[She rushes into his arms, and he embraces her repeatedly.

EUSÈBE
My wife! my wife! do I hold you in my arms!—My father!
[Throws himself on **TRICASTIN Snr**]
Oh, I did not think we should ever meet more!—My dear Amédée—my friends—
[Turning to them, then to his **FATHER** again]
Oh, my father, I thought of you, and of my wife, in the midst of all the dangers!

TRICASTIN Snr
How have you escaped? I here devote my future days to that blest Providence, who, in protecting you, has rendered those days worth preserving.

CONRAD
Relate, my friend, the particulars of what has passed.

EUSÈBE [Shrinking]
Oh, that I could forget them all—banish the whole for ever from my memory!—That all who were spectators could do the same, and human nature never be scandalized by the report!—But that's impossible—nations remote will hear it, and states of savages enroll us Fellow Citizens.

MADAME TRICASTIN
Oh, Heaven! he is wounded—behold his clothes!—

EUSÈBE [Wildly]
No, I am not wounded—these stains came from the veins—of thy mother—thy uncles—thy sisters—and all of those, who clung fast round me, and I tried in vain to defend.

MADAME TRICASTIN
Oh, horror!—yet, while you live to tell the tale, I will bear it.

CONRAD
But how preserve yourself?

EUSÈBE
By miracle—I fought with the assassins, and fell amongst my brethren—at that moment my senses left me.—When they returned, and I put out my arms to embrace my fellow sufferers, I found I clasped nothing but dead bodies.—I rose from the horrid pile, and by a lamp discerned (all gashed with wounds) faces, that but a few hours before I had seen shine with health and benevolence.—Rushing from the ghastly scene, I fled. I knew not where, about the town—my sword in my hand, reeking with blood, my hair dishevelled, and my frantic features caused me to be taken for one of the murderers, so I passed unmolested, once more to see the dearer part of my family.—But am I with them? really with them? My ideas are confused.—Poor helpless victims of ferocious vengeance, pale, convulsed with terror, and writhing under the ruffian's knife, pursue and surround me.—Am I, am I with my living family?

MADAME TRICASTIN
Thou art with me—and now the only relation I have on earth—for my sake, therefore, re-collect your scattered thoughts.

EUSÈBE
No, I still hear the shrieks of my expiring friends, mingled with the furious shouts of their triumphant foes. I saw poor females, youths, and helpless infants try to ward off the last fatal blow, then sink beneath it—I saw aged men dragged by their white hairs; a train of children following to prevent their fate, and only rush upon their own. I saw infants encouraged by the fury of their tutors, stab other infants sleeping in their cradles.*

MADAME TRICASTIN
Oh, Heavens!—

EUSÈBE
I crossed the Seine—its water blushed with blood, and bore upon its bosom disfigured bodies, still warm with life.—At the sight, single as I was, I would have attempted vengeance;—but you, my dear relations—the thought of leaving you behind, restrained the mad design.

CONRAD
Revenge is not now too late.

EUSÈBE [Taking hold of his hand]
And here let us swear—

TRICASTIN Snr
Hold—vengeance is for Heaven—by pursuing retaliation, we shall assume the power of God, and forfeit the rights of Man.

MADAME TRICASTIN
Rather lot us fly the danger which threatens us; we know the tendency of the people even of this place—the infection of the metropolis still spreads—let us leave this city—nay, the land: nor breathe its air till the sweet breeze of peace restore its lost tranquillity.

TRICASTIN Snr

My son, if your father's voice has any power; if you are not bewildered by the direful frenzy which has seized your enemies; if you have been preserved to me my child still to obey my commands, fly with your wife to a neighbouring nation, where (without coldly inquiring who is right or wrong) those in distress are sure to meet with succour.

EUSÈBE

How! fly from danger!

TRICASTIN Snr

Imprudent courage has worse effects than cowardice. Would you risk the life of your wife?

EUSÈBE

That's dearer than my own.

TRICASTIN Snr

Fly with her then, and with your children instantly. I, with these friends, will take a different route and meet you at the appointed place.

MADAME TRICASTIN [Kneeling]

My husband! Oh! if I kneel in vain to you, how can you hope my prayers will soften the murderer?

EUSÈBE

Murder!—your murderer!—protect me from the thought. I'll go with you to exile.

CONRAD

Let us retire then, and consult the means of our departure.

MENANCOURT

Eusèbe, I'll but return to my own house for a few moments, then join you here again.

[Exit.

EUSÈBE [To his **FATHER**]

You shall go with me, Sir:—I cannot, will not part company with you. No, we will go together, and console each other even under the assassin's dagger.

TRICASTIN Snr

The dagger has no terrors for me, unless 'tis pointed at your breast, my son. Call your domestics, and instantly give the necessary orders for your flight; and if, on consultation, we find it practicable, not one of us will separate from the other.

[Exeunt.

* Shocking, even to incredibility, as these murders may appear, the truth of them has been asserted in many of our public prints during the late massacre at Paris; and the same extravagant wickedness is attested to have been acted at the massacre of St. Bartholomew, by almost every historian of that time. Des enfans de dix ans tuèrent des enfans au maillot.—L'Esprit de la Ligue

ACT II

SCENE I

An Apartment at Eusèbe Tricastin's

Enter **TRICASTIN Snr**, **EUSÈBE**, and **CONRAD**, in travelling dresses.

EUSÈBE
Then, if it must be so—if it is discreet to separate—to your care, Conrad, my friend, I commit my father till we meet in England. Take every precaution possible for your safety, but let not your journeys be so rapid as to endanger his health.
[Whispering **CONRAD**]
Consider he is not so young as you, and do not suffer him to be too active, whatever inclination he may show.

TRICASTIN Snr [Cheerfully]
My boy, farewell! You will go immediately from the other door of the house, with your wife and children; and till we meet again, my blessing go along with you—the blessing of an old man, who did not think to be an exile at these years. But, in whatever country, if I meet my child, I shall not call it banishment. Are you sure you have taken money and jewels sufficient to bear you all through your journey?
[Affecting cheerfulness]
Here, take this little casket more; your wife may be in want of many things upon the road which you are not aware of: and, as for Conrad here, and myself, I'll answer for it we shall want for nothing.

EUSÈBE
Sir, I have more than enough already—paper money in abundance.

TRICASTIN Snr
But, I have been thinking, paper is doubtful currency. However, if you have no occasion for this, take it for my make—sure, at parting, Eusèbe, you cannot refuse to take a keepsake from me?

[He takes the casket.

[Enter **MADAME TRICASTIN** and **AMÉDÉE. ATTENDANTS** following with small trunks, chests, etc.

EUSÈBE
Ah! These chests will look suspicious: if it's suspected we mean to fly, we may be detained; or at least insulted. Let these be left for us at the next village.

[Enter on the opposite side **MENANCOURT** hastily.

MENANCOURT
Alas! Eusèbe Tricastin, you have saved yourself at Paris, only to fall a victim here!

TRICASTIN Snr [Starting with horror]
What do you say?

MENANCOURT
The rage of the adverse party is not confined to the capital: some from thence are arrived in this city, and have increased that flame, which has long since been kindled amongst our populace. You, young Tricastin, are proscribed; a price is set upon your life; and now the rabble are at the gate of your avenue, to claim it.

TRICASTIN Snr
I'll go to them.

EUSÈBE [Stopping him]
You go!—for what?

TRICASTIN Snr
To speak kindly to them—to let them know you have done them no harm, nor wished them any;—and it would be cruel to take an only child from an old man, who has no other comfort.

MADAME TRICASTIN
Why do we loiter?—Let us fly immediately by the other part of the house, as we had determined.

MENANCOURT
Ah, Madam, were it possible to fly, you would not see me here. The gates of the town are closed—the soldiers have declared themselves against us—a battalion guard every passage—the garrison is under arms—do you not hear the beat of the drum? That, and the sound of that bell, are the signals for a general massacre.

EUSÈBE
Then let us arm ourselves instead of meanly flying—arm, arm, and sell our blood most dearly. But where shall I conceal my wife? how protect her from their unhallowed hands? for, when I am slain, who will then fight for thee?

[Throwing his arms around her.

MENANCOURT
Give her an instrument of death to defend herself—our female enemies use them to our cost.

EUSÈBE
No, by Heaven! so Sacred do I hold the delicacy of her sex, that could she with a breath lay all our enemies dead, I would not have her feminine virtues violated by the act.
[Turning to his **FATHER**]
More sorrow still!—Those relations, who were my dearest comfort, are now the source of all my affliction!—were it not for these, I would this moment rush amongst the enemy—but you, my father, weak by age, as she by nature, can I leave you behind?

TRICASTIN Snr [Assuming a dignity]

Eusèbe, had I strength, as at your age, I would disdain to arm myself against a banditti of cowardly assassins. Besides, ought we to take away another's life, unless we had a chance to save our own? Self-preservation has here no plea; we can't preserve ourselves.

MENANCOURT
At present, they demand at this house only the life of your son; but, 'tis to be feared, when once they have forced the gate, and obtained that—

EUSÈBE
No, they would be satisfied—and they shall—with joy I go, a sacrifice for my friends.

[Going

MADAME TRICASTIN
Oh, stay, I conjure you!

TRICASTIN Snr
My son, pity your father!

MADAME TRICASTIN
Why do you hold that poniard in your hand?—do you mean to turn it against yourself? Oh! give it me.

EUSÈBE
You know not what you ask for—tremble!—touch not that dagger without suffering an anguish through every fibre! It is an eternal monument of the blackest crimes! Some drops of precious blood, never to be effaced, have spotted the steel.

MADAME TRICASTIN
You thrill me with horror—What do you mean?

EUSÈBE
Dare you ask me? I snatched it warm and reeking from the breast of your expiring mother.—
[Wildly]
I will replunge it into the hearts of those who have so well taught me how to use it.

TRICASTIN Snr
Eusèbe, you who have obeyed me through your life, will you neglect my dying words?

EUSÈBE
Your dying words!

TRICASTIN Snr
Most probably these are my last moments.—I can feel for the various passions which transport you, my child, to this excess of despair—but do not imitate your foes.—If it were left to your choice to be the murderer, or the victim, I am sure you would sooner perish than bear the name of homicide.

AMÉDÉE.
That providence which preserved you so wonderfully at Paris, may guard us here.

TRICASTIN Snr
At least, let us not render ourselves unworthy of its protection—Let us fall with courage, but with resignation—and show, in dying, we have confidence there is another life. Join hands, my children, and join me in my humble appeal to Heaven.

[They all join hands but **TRICASTIN Snr**, who comes forward and kneels.

O thou, who art all-merciful, as well as all-wise and just! look down with compassion on this weak group, who have ever walked (to the best of their understandings) in the way of thy precepts. Oh! in this moment of their calamity, save them from perishing!—Disarm their enemies!—We hope in thee—We bless thee, whether under the sword of our assailants, or restored to peace and happiness.

MADAME TRICASTIN [Kneeling]
O Heaven! preserve my husband, my children, and my father!

EUSÈBE [Kneeling]
Heaven! save my wife, my father, my children, and these my friends.

[Enter a **DOMESTIC**.

DOMESTIC
In vain have we endeavoured to guard the outward gate; the populace have forced it, and are now rushing into the house demanding my young master—Oh, sir, for mercy's sake, fly.

TRICASTIN Snr
Son, you have just now addressed yourself to the throne of heaven; and it would be mockery so noon to offend against it. Retire then, at a father's command, nor show yourself to the people till they break to your inner apartments. I will speak to them here—I have done some charitable offices, in my time, to many of our citizens—I am not the object of their pursuit—therefore, permit me to expostulate just a few moments with them—a kind word has sometimes done, with most ferocious enemies, more than a thousand swords.
[Raising his voice with passion and firmness]
Leave me to speak to them, I do command you.

MENANCOURT
He advises well.

CONRAD [To **EUSÈBE**]
My friend, retire.

MADAME TRICASTIN
Oh! obey your father, and save his life and mine.

CONRAD
Force, force him away

[CONRAD and **MENANCOURT** force him off, overcome by his various passions— **MADAME TRICASTIN**, Amédée, and the **DOMESTICS** follow, and leave only **TRICASTIN Snr** on the stage.

[Enter **GURET**, followed by **TWO OR THREE LEADERS**, such as himself, and a number of **RABBLE**, dressed like inferior tradesmen.

GURET
Where in Eusèbe Tricastin? We want Tricastin.

TRICASTIN Snr
I am he.

GURET
Are you Eusèbe Tricastin?

TRICASTIN Snr
I am.

GURET [To his **FOLLOWERS**]
They told me he was young. Is this the man?

TRICASTIN Snr
I know not who, my friends, just at this time, would willingly put himself in the place of him you ask for.

GURET
That's true.
[To his **FOLLOWERS**]
This is the man then?

1st FOLLOWER
He is like him, as well as I can remember;—yet he looks too old.

TRICASTIN Snr
Care alters men much, good sir.

2nd FOLLOWER [Coming round **TRICASTIN Snr**, and looking hard at him]
This man must be too old for him. His hair is white.

TRICASTIN Snr
Did you never hear of fright changing a young man's hair from brown to gray? and I must own—
[Affecting to tremble]
—you have frightened me a good deal, gentlemen.

GURET
If you are Eusèbe, we are come to try, and to condemn you to death.

TRICASTIN Snr
Hush—silence—

[In a low voice]
I have relations in the next room, whom it would grieve to hear you say so. Take me from this house, and then dispose of me as you think fit. Hush, hush—no noise—I go willingly with you.

GURET
Come along then—and in the open hall in the market-place, you shall indulge the fury of the multitude

[As they are leading him off, enter **EUSÈBE** on the other side.

EUSÈBE
Hold your profane hands—The fiend, who offers violence to my father—

GURET
This is then the son—seize him, my friends.

[They seize him.

1st FOLLOWER
Yes, this is young Tricastin—I now perceive this is the man we came for.

[Enter **MADAME TRICASTIN, CONRAD, MENANCOURT**, and several **ATTENDANTS**, on one side, and **DUGAS** on the other.

DUGAS
My friends, I am come with fresh instructions—Secure not only the younger Tricastin, but his whole family; and take them to the appointed place. Don't give way to your vengeance here—but there, in the midst of all our fellow-citizens, the example will be more terrible.

[They are **ALL** seized.

[Exit **DUGAS**.

EUSÈBE
Villains, let go that lady.

[Breaking from the **PERSONS** who hold him.

MADAME TRICASTIN
No, be kind and take me with him to death.

EUSÈBE [To those who hold her]
Permit me to speak a single word to this lady.
[Takes her aside]
My life, by all the tenderness I have ever shown you, save yourself for your children's sake. What will become of them when their father is gone? You have a moment now—retire, and secrete yourself among your domestics—we may yet escape by our valour; but what will avail my security if you should fall a prey? Our cruellest enemy, the man who knows us all intimately (Dugas), is this moment gone forward, off his guard, and an imposition may pass.

[To the **PERSONS** who, had seized her]
This female, gentlemen, is but an humble visitor at my house, let her retire in safety. Here's myself, my father, and my two friends, do not ask your clemency.

DOMESTIC
We'll bear the stranger in, sir, and see her safe to her own home.

[The **RABBLE** do not oppose, and the **ATTENDANTS** lead **MADAME TRICASTIN** fainting, on their shoulders, to the back of the stage.

[Re-enter **DUGAS**.

DUGAS
Regard neither struggles nor supplications, but bring them all instantly away.

[Going before.

TRICASTIN Snr [Laying hold of his hand]
Dugas, hesitate an instant, and consider once—once call to mind, before you drag me and my wretched family to immediate death, that you and I are fellow-creatures—we are countrymen—nay more, townsmen—and, till this unhappy period, have always lived like neighbours. Many little acts of friendship have passed between us—such, my neighbour, as ought not to be forgotten in an hour of tribulation like this. Oh! by the many times we have exchanged the friendly salutation of good morrow, or the kind farewell of good night—the numerous times that, at the hospitable board, we have wished each other, in our cheerful glasses, health and many a happy day!'—by all these little kindnesses, which have their weight, with minds susceptible, do not imbrue your hand in your neighbour's blood.

DUGAS.
The neighbour who thinks differently from me, I am his enemy.

TRICASTIN Snr
Lead on then—for, in that case, I rejoice you are not my friend.

[Exit **DUGAS**, followed by **TRICASTIN Snr**, **EUSÈBE**, **CONRAD**, and **MENANCOURT**, who are surrounded by the **RABBLE**.—**MADAME TRICASTIN** is taken off, by her **ATTENDANTS**, on the opposite side, as by stealth.

ACT III

SCENE I

A Street

Enter **CLEVARD** and **THEVENIN**.

THEVENIN

Oh! Clevard, my heart is sinking within me. I met, this moment, leading to a mock trial, (where Glandève, strong in the opposite party, sits as judge,) all the unhappy family of old Tricastin—this city cannot boast a more virtuous man—ungrateful people! to whom he has been a friend, a parent.— There's not an indigent man in this whole town that ever implored his help in vain; and I now behold those very villains, whom his late bounty fed, reviling him as he passes along.

CLEVARD
But this he has strength of mind to bear, no doubt, with dignity?

THEVENIN.
Unless when he turns towards his son, who follows close behind—then I can see his countenance change, the tears gush to his eyes, and stream down his furrowed cheeks. At this the rabble triumph!

[Several shouts are heard.

CLEVARD
They are coming this way; I'll join them, and be a spectator of all that passes.

THEVENIN.
I would as soon be—a sufferer.

[Exeunt severally.

SCENE II

A Hall, or large Chamber

GLANDÈVE sitting as President; a **CROWD OF PERSONS** attending.

GLANDÈVE
You have done me honour, brother citizens, in selecting me for Judge on this occasion; and, I trust, all my decrees will do honour to the confidence you have placed.

[A shout from the rabble without; after which, enter **DUGAS** and **GURET**, followed by **TRICASTIN Snr**, and all those, except **MADAME TRICASTIN** and her **ATTENDENTS**, who concluded the preceding Act.

DUGAS
President, here is a family whom I accuse of being traitors.

GLANDÈVE
Put each, in his turn, to the bar.

DUGAS
This is Tricastin the elder.

[Putting him forward.

GLANDÈVE [After a pause]
A few days ago, when I inquired, you told me, Dugas, you knew this man to be a peaceable citizen.

DUGAS
I have since changed my mind.

GLANDÈVE
Then, what do you think, my friends,—
[To the **SPECTATORS**]
—is it not better that we wait a few days longer before we put Tricastin on his trial? for in that time the witness may possibly change his mind again.

DUGAS
No, I am fixed.

GLANDÈVE
And so am I, to wait.—Officers, take the prisoner into your custody; and on your duty protect him from all violence, till I and my friends here call for him to appear.

[He is taken to the other side of the hall.

DUGAS
I thought, Glandève, you were the sworn friend of Liberty?

GLANDÈVE
And so I am—Liberty, I worship.—But, my friends, 'tis liberty to do good, not ill—liberty joined with peace and charity.

DUGAS
But, if you mean to protect the father, you surely cannot think to save the son?
[Placing him forward]
Every one present knows the crimes of Eusèbe.

GLANDÈVE
What are they?

DUGAS
All know—he does not think with us.

GLANDÈVE
And how long (answer me, some of my friends,) has it been a capital offence to think as you please? If I am a friend to freedom, my first object is, freedom of thought

DUGAS
Do you then dispute the voice of the people? 'Tis they, who relying on the wisdom of their leaders, demand the forfeit life of those who are pointed out.—Orders, received from persons authorised to give them, should be implicitly obeyed.

GLANDÈVE
This reasoning accords with military rules, when an army is prepared to give an enemy battle—but, suppose there should be issued an order for such an army to turn against itself, and each man slay his brother soldier; I trust, I hope, they would all imagine some fatal frenzy had seized the commander-in-chief, and every one lay down his arms, rather than massacre his comrade.

DUGAS
But if there are amongst them culprits to punish—

GLANDÈVE
Their trials should be conducted with all due form—a sedate dignity preside over the whole—the judge be studied in all points of law, and every supposed enemy expelled the jury. But here, a frantic whim directs the most momentous parts:—a judge is elected with no other qualification than being deemed the prisoners' adversary—the jury has the self-same recommendation.—Unthinking man! know you what you are doing? That rash, that ignorant tribunal which beheads your foe to-day, may hang you up to-morrow.

[He rises and comes forward to **TRICASTIN Snr** and his **PARTY**.

My fellow-citizens! disperse your fears—I accepted the office of judge, not to condemn, but to preserve you; and these—
[Pointing to the **PERSONS** attending in court]
—are a chosen set of men, whom I convened for the purpose of defeating the blind fury of your enemies.

TRICASTIN Snr
Virtuous Glandève! who, from a supposed adversary, art become a saviour! behold me and my son at your feet, acknowledging our admiration and our gratitude.

[They kneel.

EUSÈBE
I here dedicate to you the remainder of my life—mine, and my infant children's.

DUGAS
Glandève, you are now, by your own confession, surrounded by men whom you have packed for your purpose: but I have friends without, treble their number; and when I give the word, so far from protecting these traitors, you'll not be able to defend yourself.

GLANDÈVE
Wicked man! I scorn your power.

DUGAS [Calling with a loud voice at the side of the scenes]
Advance, my friends!—we are betrayed!—force in, and take your vengeance!

EUSÈBE
Barbarous villain! here end your crimes.

[He draws his dagger, and runs swiftly to **DUGAS** to stab him; **GLANDÈVE** flies to **DUGAS**, and screens him with his own person.

GLANDÈVE [To **EUSÈBE**]
Vindictive man, hold!—Rather strike here!
[To his own breast]
—for I trust in heaven I am less unprepared to die than he.

DUGAS [Aside]
Protected by him!

EUSÈBE
I blush at my mistaken zeal; and at your feet, noble Glandève, resign that instrument of death which I had sworn never to part from.

DUGAS
And at this moment it might be of use to you; for, behold these soldiers, who are under my command.

[A band of **SOLDIERS**, with **COLONEL ROCHELLE** at their head, instantly rush in.

DUGAS [To the **COLONEL**]
Well, Sir, you and your brave men have, I find, received my orders, and my signal for entering here. These are all your victims.

COLONEL ROCHELLE
Yes, Sir, my brave men have received your commands; and this is their brave reply:—They are all men of courage—all ready to enter the field of battle against an insulting foe, and boldly kill him; but, amongst the whole battalion, we have not one hangman. *

GLANDÈVE
They are my soldiers then, and no longer yours.
[To **DUGAS**]
—My generous men,—
[To the **SOLDIERS**]
—fly through the town, and instantly protect all those of the persecuted party!

COLONEL ROCHELLE
That we have done already, and have recovered dead corses of many from the ferocious mob. Here, close to the door of this hall, stretched on a bier, my soldiers bear a lovely matron butchered, with her two children by her side—we snatched her from the hands of her assassins before her beauteous body was disfigured: and lest they should regain it from our possession, I ordered the corpse (followed by her mournful attendants) to be surrounded by a party of our men, till we had leisure to deposit it in the family burial-place.

[A bier is brought in, followed by several domestic **ATTENDANTS** and some **SOLDIERS**.—On the bier is laid the dead body of **MADAME TRICASTIN**, and **TWO CHILDREN** dead, by her side. **EUSÈBE** stands like a statue of horror at the sight.—After the bier has been set down a little time, he goes to it.

EUSÈBE
For what have I been preserved? Oh! night that I escaped through torrents of blood, at Paris—far, far less horrible than this day to me! Father, behold your grand-children by their mother's side, and own your son was born for greater anguish than human nature can support!

COLONEL ROCHELLE [Going slowly, respectfully, and timidly up to **EUSÈBE**]
This distraction makes me not doubt but you are the unhappy father of these infants, and husband of this lady. I was so fortunate as to be some consolation to her in her last moments, and received her parting words. The crowd had entered and encompassed your house, and she had called repeatedly for assistance before I was able to make a passage to her through the multitude:—when I did, her desire to save her life had subsided; for, she had beheld her two children slain. The eldest, to the last, she held fast by the band—the youngest she pressed violently to her bosom, and, struggling to preserve, received the murderer's blow through its breast, to her own. Tell Eusèbe (she cried as I came up) I die contented, with my children; and entreat him not to grieve at what he may think I suffered at my death; for my pain, except for him I leave behind, is trivial.

EUSÈBE
Dying saint! This was to calm my despair.

TRICASTIN Snr—[To **GLANDÈVE**]
And suffer it to have its effects. I know and feel your loss, my son, and I feel my own. Oh! had she been but under this good man's shelter—

CONRAD
But when was joy superlative? Our unlooked-for release from death had been happiness supreme, but for this abatement.

GLANDÈVE
My friends, I conjure you to take every care that the perpetrators of this barbarous outrage are secured. This man—
[To **DUGAS**]
—and his, followers shall be made prisoners till our researches prove successful.—Then, the good (of all parties) will conspire to extirpate such monsters from the earth. It is not party principles which cause this devastation; 'tis want of sense—'tis guilt—for the first precept in our Christian laws is charity—the next obligation—to extend that charity EVEN TO OUR ENEMIES.

[The bier is carried off in slow procession— **TRICASTIN Snr** and **EUSÈBE** following as mourners, and the **ATTENDANTS** singing a dirge.

* A well-known reply sent by a commander, to the orders be had received from Court at the massacre of St. Bartholomew: 'Dans tout le militaire, il ne s'est trouvé que des hommes courageux, prîts à voler aux actions les plus périlleuses, mais pas un seul bourreau'.

Mrs Inchbald – A Short Biography

Elizabeth Simpson was born on 15th October 1753 at Stanningfield, near Bury St Edmunds, Suffolk. She was the eighth of nine children to John Simpson, a farmer, and his wife, Mary, née Rushbrook. The family were Roman Catholics.

Her brother was educated at school, but Elizabeth, like her sisters, was educated at home. Elizabeth also suffered from a speech impediment, a stammer.

Elizabeth's father had died when she was only eight, leaving her mother to take care of a large family. These were difficult times.

Despite the fact that she suffered from a debilitating stammer she was determined, from a very young age, to become an actress. She had loved theatre from her very first childhood visit.

As a young woman Elizabeth was tall and slender. But this beauty brought with it the many attentions of men. It was double-edged.

Elizabeth had written to the manager of the Norwich Theatre to obtain acting work. He had replied that he would welcome a visit for her to audition. For her young naïve years this seemed like a golden opportunity. However, in 1770 her family forbade her attempt to take on an acting assignment there. They had no such qualms with her brother George, who entered the acting profession.

In April 1772, Elizabeth left, without permission, for London to pursue her chosen career. Although she was successful in obtaining parts her audiences found it difficult to admire her talents given her speech impediment. However, Elizabeth was diligent and hard-working on attempting to overcome this hurdle. She spent much time concentrating on pronunciation in order to eliminate the stammer. She was known to write out the parts she wanted to perform and practice the lines to point of such familiarity that her impediment was banished. Her acting, although at times stilted, especially in monologues, gained praise for her approach, and for her well-developed characters. For the audience she came across as a real person, not just an actor performing a piece. Elizabeth would keenly study the performances of others before she herself performed.

In these early months Elizabeth was young and alone, and reportedly also suffered from the attentions of sexual predators.

In June, merely two months after arriving she accepted an offer of marriage from Joseph Inchbald, a fellow Catholic and actor. They had met before on her previous trips to London, usually to see her brother, George, acting on stage. He had written her several letters proposing marriage which she had declined. But now it seemed the most expedient way to make progress in her career.

By all accounts it was still an odd choice. Joseph was a so-so actor, and at least twice her age as well as being the father of two illegitimate sons. The marriage was to produce no children and was not the happiest of unions.

On 4th September of that year, 1772, Elizabeth and Joseph appeared for the first time together on stage in 'King Lear'. The following month they toured Scotland with the West Digges's theatre company. This was to continue for the next four years.

In 1776 they decided on a change of career and a change of country. They moved to France. Joseph would now learn to paint, and Elizabeth would study French. It was a short-lived disaster. Within a month all their funds were gone and a return to England was necessitated.

They moved to Liverpool, Canterbury and Yorkshire and acted for both the Joseph Younger's company and Tate Wilkinson's company in search of permanency and a recovery from their ill-fortune.

Completely unexpectedly Joseph died in June 1779. Despite her loss Elizabeth continued to perform across the country from Dublin to London and places in between.

In 1780, she joined the Covent Garden Company and played Bellarion in 'Philaster'.

In all Elizabeth's acting career was only moderately successful and lasted some 17 years. However, she appeared in many classical roles as well as new plays such as Hannah Cowley's 'The Belle's Stratagem'. Around the theatre she was known for upholding high moral standards. She later described having to fend off sexual advances from, among others, stage manager James Dodd and theatre manager John Taylor.

It was now in the years after her husband's death that that Elizabeth decided on a new literary path. With no attachments, and acting taking up only some of her time, she decided to write plays.

Her first play to be performed was 'A Mogul Tale or, The Descent of the Balloon', in 1784, in which she also played the leading female role of Selina. The play was premiered at the Haymarket Theatre.

'Lovers' Vows', in 1798, was based on her translation of August von Kotzebues original work and garnered both praise and complements from Jane Austen and was featured as a focus of moral controversy in her novel Mansfield Park. Although Austen's book brought more fame to Elizabeth, 'Lovers' Vows' initially ran for only forty-two nights when originally performed in 1798.

One of the things that separated Elizabeth from other contemporary playwrights was her ability to translate plays from German and French into English and to use them as a foundation. These translations were popular with the public and her talents in bringing the characters to life was instrumental in achieving this.

Her success as a playwright enabled Elizabeth to support herself and not need a new husband to carry out this role. Between 1784 and 1805 she had 19 of her comedies, sentimental dramas, and farces (many of them translations from the French) performed at London theatres, although it is thought she actually wrote between 21 and 23 in total depending on which account you think is most accurate. She is usually credited as Mrs Inchbald.

As well she wrote two novels; 'A Simple Story' was published in 1791 and once referred to as "the most elegant English fiction of the eighteenth century". 'Nature and Art' was published in 1796. Both have been constantly reprinted.

Her four-volume autobiography was destroyed before her death upon the advice of her confessor, but she left a few of her diaries.

In her later years she found time to do a considerable amount of editorial and critical work. In 1805, she decided to try being a theatre critic. This literary excursion, after the praise for her acting and more so for her writing, seemed to be a low point in her achievements. The reception to her work amongst her peer critics was low, one commented upon her ignorance of Shakespeare.

Her career from actress, to playwright and novelist was achieved in difficult times for women to accomplish such things. Indeed, whilst the theatre and its boundaries were quite strict she managed, in her novels, to explore political radicalism. Her good looks together with her passionate and fiery nature attracted a string of admirers but she never re-married. Despite her love of independence, she still desired and sought social respectability.

Mrs Elizabeth Inchbald died on 1st August 1821 in Kensington, London.

She is buried in the churchyard of St Mary Abbots. On her gravestone is written, "Whose writings will be cherished while truth, simplicity, and feelings, command public admiration."

Mrs Inchbald – A Concise Bibliography

Plays
Mogul Tale; or, The Descent of the Balloon (1784)
Appearance is against Them (1785)
I'll Tell you What (1785)
The Widow's Vow (1786)
The Midnight Hour (1787)
Such Things Are (1787)
All on a Summer's Day (1787)
Animal Magnetism (c1788)
The Child of Nature (1788)
The Married Man (1789)
Next Door Neighbours (1791)
Everyone has his Fault (1793)
To Marry, or not to Marry (1793)
The Wedding Day (1794)
Wives as They Were and Maids as They Are (1797)
Lovers' Vows (1798)
The Wise Man of the East (1799)
The Massacre (1792 (not performed)
A Case of Conscience (published 1833)
The Ancient Law (not performed)
The Hue and Cry (unpublished)
Young Men and Old Women (Lovers No Conjurers) (adaptation of Le Méchant; unpublished)

Novels

A Simple Story (1791)

Nature and Art (1796)

www.ingramcontent.com/pod-product-compliance
Lightning Source LLC
Chambersburg PA
CBHW021950040426
42448CB00008B/1333

CONTENTS